Exploring Materials

Plastic

Abby Colich

Heinemann
LIBRARY
Chicago, Illinois

© 2014 Heinemann Library
an imprint of Capstone Global Library, LLC
Chicago, Illinois

To contact Capstone Global Library please phone 800-747-4992, or visit our website www.capstonepub.com

Edited by Abby Colich, Daniel Nunn, and Catherine Veitch
Designed by Marcus Bell
Picture research by Tracy Cummins
Production by Victoria Fitzgerald
Originated by Capstone Global Library Ltd

Library of Congress Cataloging-in-Publication Data
Colich, Abby.
  Plastic / Abby Colich.
      pages cm.—(Exploring materials)
  Includes bibliographical references and index.
  ISBN 978-1-4329-8017-7 (hb)—ISBN 978-1-4329-8025-2 (pb) 1.
Plastics—Juvenile literature. I. Title.

TP1125.C65 2014
668.4—dc23   2012047492

Acknowledgments
We would like to thank the following for permission to reproduce photographs: Alamy: Ronald Karpilo, 11; Getty Images: altrendo images, 18, Jose Luis Pelaez Inc, 7, 14, Jupiterimages, 10, 23 bottom, Klaus Tiedge, cover, Win McNamee, 9, 23 middle; iStockphoto: aydinmutlu, 8, Image Source, 4, Juanmonino, 19; Shutterstock: Africa Studio, 22 top right, Alexander Dashewsky, 6 top right, Alinute Silzeviciute, 5, Chamille White, 20, Denis Vrublevsk, 22 top left, Dmitriy Shironosov, 12, Gualberto Becerra, 6 top left, Jari Hindstroem, 13, Kostenko Maxim, 22 bottom, krugloff, 6 bottom right, Michaelstockfoto, 6 bottom left, Photogrape, 21, Stocksnapper, 17, 23 top, VIPDesignUSA, back cover, 15, Tetra Images, 16

We would like to thank Valarie Akerson, Nancy Harris, Dee Reid, and Diana Bentley for their invaluable help in the preparation of this book.

Every effort has been made to contact copyright holders of any material reproduced in this book. Any omissions will be rectified in subsequent printings if notice is given to the publisher.

Contents

What is Plastic?

Plastic is a material.

Materials are what things are made from.

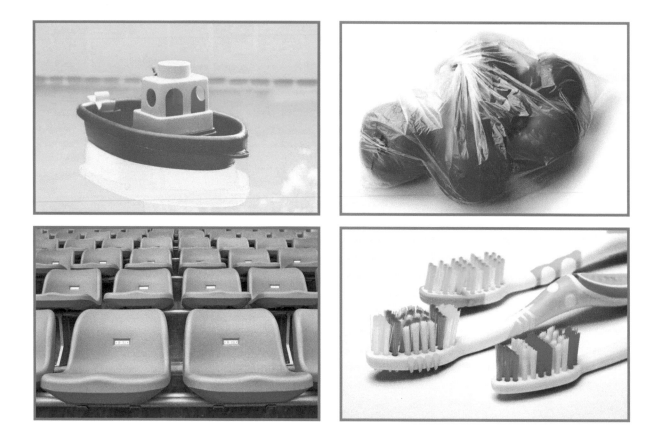

Plastic has many uses.

We use plastic to make many
different things.

Where Does Plastic Come From?

Plastic is made by people.

oil

Plastic is made from oil.

Plastic can be recycled or reused.

Recycled plastic can be used to make new things.

What Is Plastic Like?

Plastic can be colored or clear.

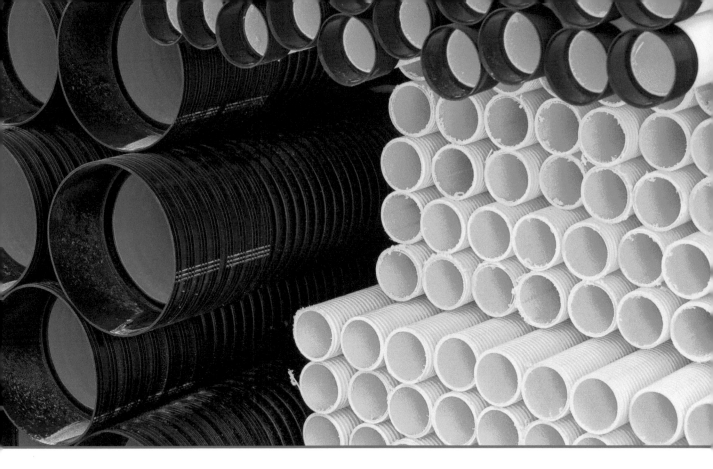

Plastic can be thick or thin.

smooth →

Plastic can be smooth or bumpy.

Plastic can bend and change shape.

How Do We Use Plastic?

We use plastic when we eat and drink.

container →

We use plastic containers to store things

Some toys are made from plastic.

Some bags are made from plastic.

bicycle helmet

sunglasses

Plastic can keep us safe

Plastic is used in many places.

Quiz

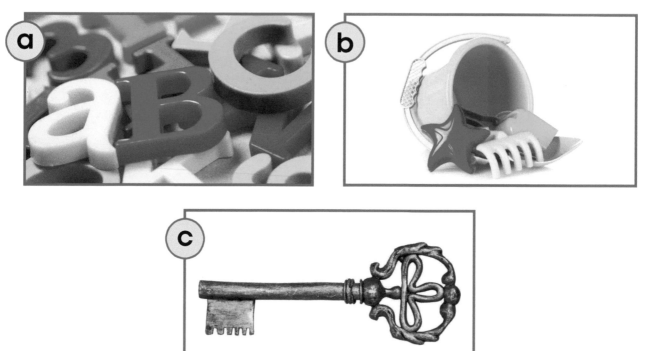

Which of these things are made from plastic?

Answer on page 24.

Picture glossary

container something used to store things

oil slippery liquid that does not mix with water

recycle make used items into new things

Index

The **letters (a)** and **beach toys (b)** are made from plastic.

Notes for parents and teachers

Before reading

Ask children if they have heard the term "material" and what they think it means. Reinforce the concept of materials. Explain that all objects are made from different materials. A material is something that takes up space and can be used to make other things. Ask children to give examples of different materials. These may include glass, plastic, and rubber.

To get children interested in the topic, ask if they know what plastic is. Identify any misconceptions they may have. Ask them to think about whether their ideas might change as the book is read.

After reading

• Check to see if any of the identified misconceptions have changed.

• Show the children examples of plastic, including plastic toys, bags, and bottles.

• Pass the plastic objects around. Ask the children to describe the properties of each object. What color is it? Is it hard? Does it bend? Is it heavy or light? Ask them to name other items made from plastic.